Celebrating Friendsgiving

Date

_____

D1727829

Location

_____

Friends in Attendance

Friends in Attendance

Friends in Attendance

Guest

_____

Thankful For

_____

_____

_____

_____

_____

Guest

_____

Thankful For

_____

_____

_____

_____

_____

Guest

_____

Thankful For

_____

_____

_____

_____

_____

Guest

_____

Thankful For

_____

_____

_____

_____

_____

Guest

_____

Thankful For

_____

_____

_____

_____

_____

_____

Guest

_____

Thankful For

_____

_____

_____

_____

_____

_____

Guest

_____

Thankful For

_____

_____

_____

_____

_____

Guest

_____

Thankful For

_____

_____

_____

_____

_____

Guest

_____

Thankful For

_____

_____

_____

_____

_____

Guest

_____

Thankful For

_____

_____

_____

_____

_____

Guest

_____

Thankful For

_____

_____

_____

_____

_____

Guest

_____

Thankful For

_____

_____

_____

_____

_____

_____

Guest

_____

Thankful For

_____

_____

_____

_____

_____

Guest

_____

Thankful For

Guest

_____

Thankful For

_____

_____

_____

_____

_____

Guest

_____

Thankful For

_____

_____

_____

_____

_____

Guest

_____

Thankful For

_____

_____

_____

_____

_____

_____

Guest

_____

Thankful For

_____

_____

_____

_____

_____

Guest

_____

Thankful For

_____

_____

_____

_____

_____

Guest

_____

Thankful For

_____

_____

_____

_____

_____

Guest

_____

Thankful For

_____

_____

_____

_____

_____

Guest

_____

Thankful For

_____

_____

_____

_____

_____

Guest

_____

Thankful For

Guest

_____

Thankful For

_____

_____

_____

_____

_____

Guest

_____

Thankful For

_____

_____

_____

_____

_____

Guest

_____

Thankful For

_____

_____

_____

_____

_____

_____

Guest

_____

Thankful For

_____

_____

_____

_____

_____

Guest

_____

Thankful For

_____

_____

_____

_____

_____

_____

Guest

_____

Thankful For

_____

_____

_____

_____

_____

Guest

_____

Thankful For

Guest

_____

Thankful For

_____

_____

_____

_____

_____

_____

Guest

_____

Thankful For

_____

_____

_____

_____

_____

_____

Guest

_____

Thankful For

_____

_____

_____

_____

_____

Guest

_____

Thankful For

_____

_____

_____

_____

_____

Guest

_____

Thankful For

_____

_____

_____

_____

_____

Guest

_____

Thankful For

_____

_____

_____

_____

_____

Guest

_____

Thankful For

_____

_____

_____

_____

_____

_____

Guest

_____

Thankful For

_____

_____

_____

_____

_____

Guest

_____

Thankful For

_____

_____

_____

_____

_____

Guest

_____

Thankful For

_____

_____

_____

_____

_____

Guest

_____

Thankful For

_____

_____

_____

_____

_____

Guest

_____

Thankful For

_____

_____

_____

_____

_____

Guest

Thankful For

Guest

_____

Thankful For

_____

_____

_____

_____

_____

Guest

_____

Thankful For

_____

_____

_____

_____

_____

Guest

_____

Thankful For

_____

_____

_____

_____

_____

Guest

_____

Thankful For

_____

_____

_____

_____

_____

Guest

_____

Thankful For

_____

_____

_____

_____

_____

Guest

_____

Thankful For

_____

_____

_____

_____

_____

_____

Guest

_____

Thankful For

_____

_____

_____

_____

_____

_____

Printed in Poland
by Amazon Fulfillment
Poland Sp. z o.o., Wrocław

28568588R00061